INK AND DREAMS: TEENAGE MUSINGS

A BOUTIQUE POETRY COLLECTION

RENA TARA PHOOKAN

Made with ♥ on the Notion Press Platform
www.notionpress.com

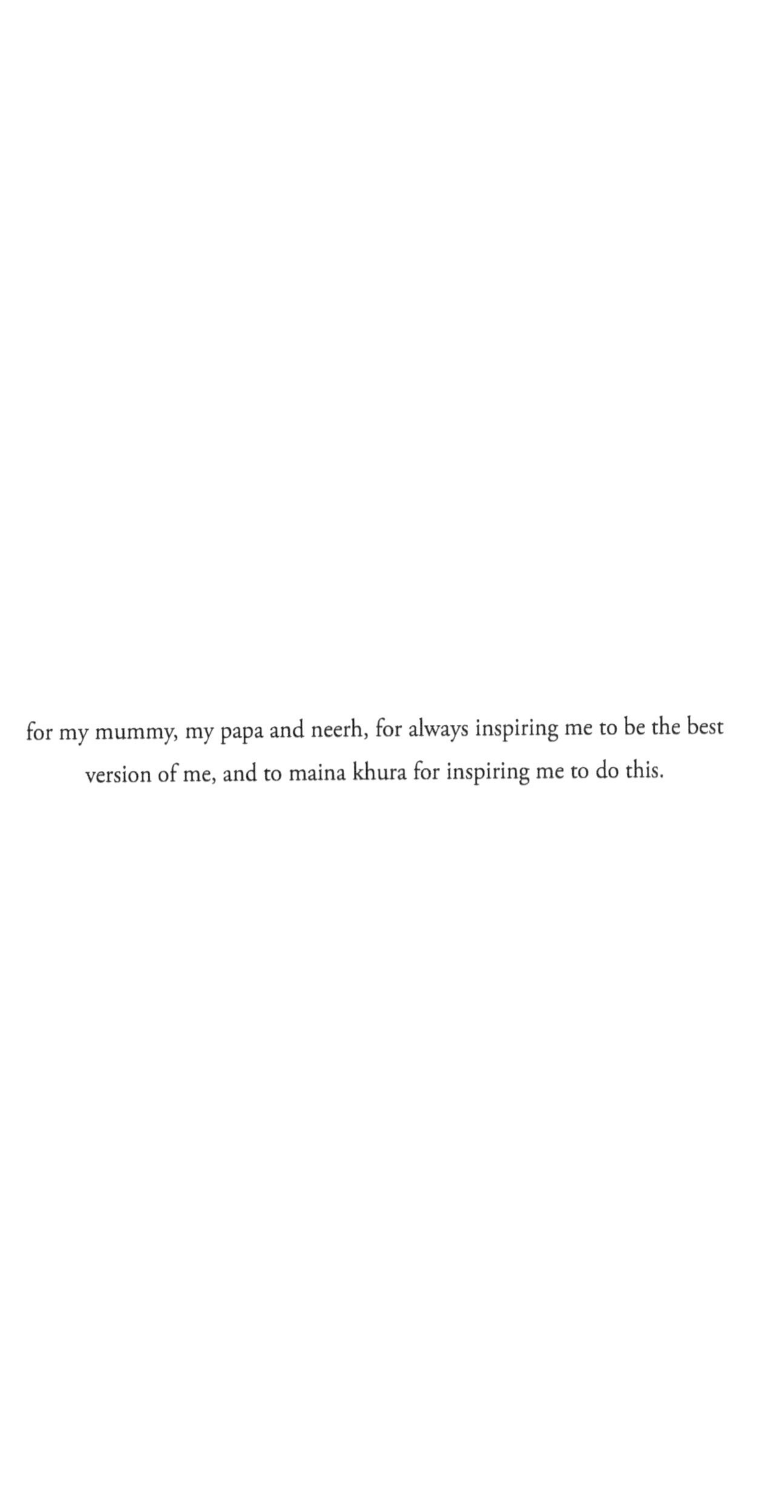

for my mummy, my papa and neerh, for always inspiring me to be the best version of me, and to maina khura for inspiring me to do this.

Contents

Foreword

this began as an unexpected journey, that started around mid november 2023, when i decided i wanted to publish a few poems id written over the course of the past few years.

the moment i sat down and started flicking through my collection, i knew i wanted to do this as early on in 2024 as possible. my inspiration came from my uncle - sanjit phukan, who has already published two phenomenal books of poetry, and is one of the most creative people ive ever known.

im proud to say this has been my first ever complete solo achievement, with no hand holding from anyone around me. im filled with a deep sense of pride, excitement and nervousness as i write this.

ive always expressed myself through writing, and i hope this little collection of 13 poems is something you might relate to.

so, from my heart to yours,

here is Ink and Dreams : Teenage Musings.

Acknowledgements

my mother, for inspiring me to read from an early age

my father, for telling me bedtime stories almost every other day

my brother, who encouraged me to be creative by making me come up with new stories for him every day,

my uncle, for being an example of immense creativity,

bali aunty, for guiding me through this process,

and to my koka and dadai, for always teaching me to live with grace.

Prologue

In the pages that follow, explore the poignant verses penned by a young soul navigating the tumultuous landscape of adolescence. This poetry book delves into the intricate tapestry of body image, loss, love, and the profound journey of growing up. Through the lens of heartfelt words, witness the struggles and triumphs of friendship, as the author fearlessly bares their soul, inviting you to find solace and resonance within these lines

1. on growing up

i have grown, mother, i have grown.

i long to feel the same comfort i did in your arms, listening to that soft whisper of your voice telling me its all going to be okay.

i have grown father, i have grown.

i long to catch that cricket ball once again, to feel the weight of the badminton racquet in my hands as you shout, "i need you to put more power into your serve" and i smile because i adore spending time with you.

i have grown brother, i have grown.

i was always older, and i long to protect you from the evils of the world.

i long for those nights when we'd watch our favourite show together or laugh ourselves silly over something trivial.

now, i hold you mother, as you shed tears in my arms over the loss of your own father.

now, i do not play with you as much father, for i see how quickly you lose your breath, and how your back gives way much quicker.

now, i watch brother, as you tell me about minecraft and some youtuber i have never heard of, and i realize that twinkle comics and mr men stories won't do.

i have grown my loves, i've grown.

but now i realize, so have you.

for my mom, dad and brother

2. the new reflection

i looked at the mirror today
and surprisingly i didn't dislike what i saw.
i didn't criticize my hips,
or my tummy
i didn't feel frustration at the shape of my dips.
i admired my marks, my freckles and operation scar
i smiled when i traced the uneven line, a memory of when i was nine.
i didn't wish i looked like a skinny star
i didn't wish for my diet to start performing miracles.
i didn't expect my body, my body that has been with me all throughout
to look like one that was printed in magazines.
i looked at the mirror and i smiled at what i saw.
is this what healing feels like?
is this what is feels like to be free of self hate?
is this how it feels to begin to love yourself?
because if it is, i want it.
i have learned a little late to accept what i am
but i am working, working hard, till im ecstatic with what i see.
but hey, you know what?
i think I like me.

3. on friendships

friendships fall apart
crash and burn
left to die.
and yet, despite it all, i wonder,
should i text? should i call?
should i be the one to take the first step?
my ego stops me. my pride stops me.
the hurt in my heart stops me.
but still, i text.
i call.
because if i am not kind, if i am not nice,
there is nothing left to define who i am.

4. "try, try, try again"

If at first you don't succeed,
Try try try again.
When life doesn't give you what you desperately need,
Try try try again.
When you need a break that just can't seem to come,
Try try try again.
When you feel so low and down in the dumps,
Take a step back
Breathe in
Breathe out
Relax.
As one door closes, another door opens.
And your much needed break will find you,
Whether in the roar of the ocean waves or the serenity of the cold
mountains,
It will find you,
So try try try again.

5. we watch the sunrise

We watch as it rises on the horizon,

Signalling the start of a brand new day.

And with a smile and a sigh,

We put our books away.

We watch the sun set,

And the darkness of nightfall descends,

"Don't fret" says the career counselor, with a comforting smile,

"You'll get into the college of your dreams" she says,

But that doesn't quell the fears of our minds.

We watch the moon rise,

Tired eyes looking at the clock and wishing desperately that we could

turn back time.

Our papers lie astray, in every nook and corner,

We groan and moan and complete the work we've been putting off,

And go back to studying the works

of Hemingway, Woolf, and Warner.

We bite our lips raw, feet tapping nervously against the concrete floor,

As the examiner passes around the pieces of paper that determine

whether you're gonna whoop in happiness or walk in tears out the

door.

And the gnawing fear rises, and as does the numbing pain,

"What if it wasn't good enough,"

"What if I wasn't good enough"

"Am i doomed to being a failure for the rest of my life because I failed

to get a A?"

We watch as the sun rises, slowly illuminating the glistening tears shed
in the dark of night, suppressed sobs hiding the shame.
The shame of not doing well enough,
The fear of not being good enough,
The desperation of wanting to be good enough.
We close our eyes.
And get ready to do it all again.

6. it's funny to think..

its funny to think we once truly knew each other.

laughed together, cried together, sang together, danced together.

its funny to think you once knew everything about me,

my fears, my hopes, my loves and my dreams.

its funny to think that once we never wanted to say goodbye to each other,

grasping our hands together and pouting for just ten more minutes to play.

its funny to think i once knew everything about you.

now, i just smile and look away.

its funny to think that once i would have given up my very soul for you, would have done anything to make you smile.

its funny to think i still would give you the world, even though you cant spare me a minute of your time.

its funny to think that i once loved you as a sister, held you as a sister, fought with you as a sister.

and yet despite the efforts, i watch as the two ticks turn blue, and minutes turn to hours, and into days and you dont respond.

its sad to think i would still fight all the evils in the world for you, hold you, protect you.

but you would only give me a formal greeting.

its sad to think that despite facing it all together,

you chose to stray away.

7. on music

i will escape in you once again, blocking out the cruelties of this world.
i will smile as hozier's melodious voice croons soft tales of love,
through my speaker as i bake.
i will listen in wondrous awe, as the eclectically stirring music of pink
floyd thrums through my headphones, as I lie awake late at night
pondering the true meaning of life.
i will pay close attention to the poetic magic of taylor swift's folklore,
that touches a spot in my heart.
i will sway as elvis' familiar voice fills the apartment one evening,
marvelling at the king of rock.
i will listen with bated breath as kun faya kun and jashn e bahaara play
in the background, eyes shut as the beauty of the words washes over
me.
i will fight back tears as i listen to the gentle twangs of a country guitar
playing tennesee whiskey or wondering why, basking in the glorious
relaxation it brings.
i will feel, the depth of my emotions through music,
because music has never left my side.

8. on loss

Sometimes I jolt awake,
Haunted by the ghost of your laugh
My breath quivers and trembles
As I recount your jovial spirit and your neverending magnanimity.
Sometimes the memories of how much you loved me and spoiled me
brings a painful lump toy throat
And no matter how hard I seem to swallow,
The heartache doesn't subside
And neither does the lingering fear that slowly,
I'm forgetting the sound of your voice.
I recall the wisdom you passed onto me,
Along with your love of books
I look upon the sleek glass shelves in your bedroom with a fond smile,
Snuggling into your bed and preparing to while my time away
listening to the cassettes you kept so perfectly.
Your glass jar of chocolate shots still sits unperturbed,
The last packet still awaiting,
But I cannot bring myself to take it away,
My heart wanting nothing more than to keep your memory alive in
every single way.
I remember the golden honey you brought to us each morning with a
spoon,
Telling us "this is good for your health"
Now i cannot look at the sugary sweet syrup without a burst of pain
in my heart,

Longing to see you walk towards me again in your cap and glasses,
telling me "khai lua, bhal hoi tumar karne"
I still remember the day I heard you were gone,
My body froze and my brain stopped comprehending information for
a mere minute
Before the numbing pain took over my bones.
Sometimes the memories slap me across the face harshly and leave me
cold and unhappy
Sometimes the memories are a gentle caress, reminding me of how
loved I was by all of you.
And all the time, the memories are a reminder that I carry you in my
blood, and must do everything I can to make you proud.
For all I can say is,
"What men, what men, what mighty good men"
for my koka, dadai and koko khura. I love you always

9. on love

never did i imagine
love could be this carefree
this giving, this warm,
as homely as it can be.
never did i imagine id smile this wide
that my cheeks would flush this red
or that you'd be my last thought
before i go to bed.

10. house no 47

In the shadows of House No.47's red brick grace,

A tale unfolds, a dwelling's lonely embrace.

Abandoned echoes of a family's scattered tune,

Whispers of joy lost, under a slanting tin monsoon.

Ivy, a green shroud, adorns the sturdy walls,

Jasmine and bougainvillea, run along them, with their comforting calls.

Tangled gardens, once a vibrant bloom,

Now a wild dance of grass and weeds, in nature's own living room.

Windows, once open wide to let in the fresh air, now veiled in dust,

Cobwebs weave memories, as precious as moondust.

Doors locked tight, locking in the past,

Time itself is shunned, as it slips by so fast.

The tin roof, once painted a lush green, now rusted with age,

Rain's tears and neglect, penned on each page.

Yet amid this unfolding decay, glimpses of beauty unfold,

Marigolds defiant, in yellows and oranges bold.

An old gardener tends to a fading dream,

Dahlias, daisies, poppies in a seasonal scheme.

Birds still sing, in nests they weave,

A lonesome crow and stray dog, memories retrieve.

House No.47, a sigh in the breeze,

Longing whispers, through the rustling trees.

A chronicle of times, of people once near,

In its silent walls, even nostalgia sheds a tear.

11. blossom of love

when you feel a winter neverending, and hope seems too far to reach,

when you've tried despite the hurting, to practice all that you preach.

when you feel so lost and lonely, sweater sleeves wipe away the tears of pain,

when all luck seems to evade you, and happiness seems to fade.

when your heart feels like its frozen, caught up in a blizzard of snow,

when the words people utter,

seem devoid of any love,

when the going gets rough, and you want to scream and shout

when all you can do is hold on, mind overcrowded with doubt.

when the promise of a brighter future is like a cloud,

just away from reach

when your own thoughts drown you ,

anxiety threatens to unleash.

when you feel all is lost, and you feel that familiar tug of hurt.

when all you do seems too less, and your words become rough and curt.

know that every night welcomes a sunrise, every bad memory begins to fade,

every blossom needs it sunlight, its nourishment to extend.

know that one day that blizzard in your heart will slowly melt away,

making space for a beautiful blossom,

petals stretching to feel the light of day.

let the seed of love enrich you, turn your darkest night to day
let its warm embrace envelop you, tell you its all going to be okay
plant the flowers of hope and happiness,
be resilient, and one day
you'll see the flowers blooming
making your pain fade away.
hold onto the ones that love you, the ones who've always stayed
and let that sadness sprout into a thing of utter beauty.
every flower needs that shower of rain
let the love bloom deep in your heart
making you strong once again
know that although things may be rough,
you will feel love again.

12. on friendships (ii)

Through thick and thin, you've been my rock,

In life's journey, an unyielding dock.

Laughs and tears, we've shared it all,

Friends like you, a constant call.

Through the years, a bond so true,

In rainy days and skies of blue.

You've had my back, through thick and thin,

I'm forever grateful for the friendship we're in.

You've seen me at my lowest

And cheered for me at my highest

Held my hand through dark days,

And loved me through the bad days.

From tiny little girls just learning to laugh and play,

To older, mature girls, navigating this world, trying not to be led astray.

Through challenges big and bold

To victories small and sweet,

Know that i'm always here for you,

As you're always there for me.

for my best friend, rusha.

13. new years

i didn't wake up on the first of this year feeling like a brand new person
i didn't wake up with a cemented new person with new hopes and
dreams and aspirations
i did make a new list of resolutions
that don't quite read like resolutions but more like a bunch of strict
rules at a museum
"eat less, work out more, get out more, wake up earlier, go to bed
sooner, eat out less, worry less"
for a person who absolutely detests maths, i spend a lot of time
subtracting things from my life,
making strict rules for myself to follow even though I'm not quite a
rule follower myself.
i spend more time creating an image of perfection than i actually do
implementing it.
all around me I see people saying this like "this year will be my year,
the best one yet" and i nod through the confusion.
what constitutes a great year?
wasn't this year a great year?
i made new friends, travelled to new places, started a new journey at a
new school and met people who changed my life for the better.
i sang more, i danced more, i laughed more i cried more.
i cooked more and experimented with art more.
i learnt how to navigate leadership and how to make the absolute
perfect vanilla butter cake.

i learnt that I don't really like the way the colour yellow looks on me, and that I really don't like nude lipstick.

i learnt that i adore red roses and that I have an obsession with detective fiction.

i learnt that I have bad anxiety and very little confidence

i learnt that I look great in black and that i can be strong when I need to be.

I learnt to let go of people who hurt me and embrace the people who love me for me.

I said goodbyes and hellos,

I love yous and i hate yous,

Burnt bridges and tried to fix them.

I ate calamari and i made Mexican food for my aunt

My dogs greeted me everytime i came home

I came home everytime

I got to try new chocolates and find a new eyeliner i really like

I got to go on so many aeroplanes and take so many aesthetic photos

I went to gym and i went to the science museum in Amsterdam.

I ticked things off my bucket list and added things to my bucket list

I wrote poems and stories and tore em up the next day and flushed them.

I don't know if I'll achieve the things on my resolutions list again

But I do know I'll do these things all over again

And next year I'll sit again, at a cafe, with my notes app open in front of me

Drinking a warm cup of coffee after promising myself to be more hydrated this year

Making another list of things to do that year and promptly forgetting to do them again.

Celebrating the end of a another beautiful year while saying "This next year, it will be mine!"

to those who've wandered through these lines,

thank you for sharing in my precious these rhymes.

end.